Early Fires

Other Works by RB Morris

Plays

The Man Who Lives Here Is Loony
A one-man play based on the life and works of James Agee

Music

Local Man
Knoxville Sessions
Take That Ride
Zeke and the Wheel
Empire

Early Fires

poems

RB Morris

Iris Press
Oak Ridge, Tennessee

Copyright © 2007 by RB Morris

All rights reserved. No portion of this book may be reproduced in any form or by any means, including electronic storage and retrieval systems, without explicit, prior written permission of the publisher, except for brief passages excerpted for review and critical purposes.

Iris Press is an imprint of the Iris Publishing Group, Inc.

www.irisbooks.com

Library of Congress Cataloging-in-Publication Data

Morris, R. B.
 Early fires : poems / R.B. Morris.
     p. cm.
 ISBN 978-0-916078-92-8 (alk. paper)
 ISBN 978-0-916078-93-5 (pbk. : alk. paper)
 1. Knoxville (Tenn.)—Poetry. I. Title.
 PS3613.O7756E17 2007
 811'.6—dc22

2007004639

Dedicated to Eric Sublett, co-editor, co-conspirator, collaborator and friend through these years.

Contents

Author's Note   10

The Man Upstairs

Return   15
Sleep   17
I Am Back   19
The Attic   21
There Was a Fire   22
A Short Sculpture of Tiné   24
You Must Bear Water   26
Fort Sanders   27
When I Was Here   28
We Are All Ghosts   30
Where Are You Now   32
Free Soup   33
There Are No Lights   35
Count   37
(PARK) (BANK) (12:12) (62°)   38
Fugitive Heart   42
Paradise   43
Crow-Morris Man   48
Crows in the City   49
Local Man   50
"The Man Who Lives Here Is Loony"   52
He Likes to Talk   53
The Man Upstairs   54
When God Dozes   57
Nails   58
the tallest wall   59
Life   60

The Ice Storm of '81   61
This Space Heater   62
A Girl Came Upstairs   63
Now As the Ancient Night   69
Song for a Changing Season   70
Eviction   72
The Man Upstairs   73
Behind Enemy Lines   76

Littoral Zone

My cousin Bobby   79
China Waits   80
Vertical Horizons   81
Gulls Turning   82
When the Pigeons Lift Up   83
Poets I Have Followed Around   86
Upon Meeting Gregory Corso   89
On the Bus   90
City   91
The Acts Man   92
Upon Meeting Prophet Wilson   94
Song for Atlantic Avenue   97
In a Lazy   98
Was it Folly   99
The Little Boy   100
There   110
The Ragman   111
go buy a cantaloupe   115
jesus is jogging   116
Bird Paths   117
How the Daylight   121
The shadows of the pelicans   122

Lost Pavilion

How Do You Fare   125
Alley des Refusés   129
What City   130
Tic toc town for the taker   130
man wants to walk   132
My Vowels Are Other Colors Than Arthur Rimbaud's   133
Knoxville the gray lost   135
Fog Lifted Off   136
The L&N Hotel   138
Bridge Avenue   139
When My Brother Comes Stumbling   146
Father Fisheye   149
Reverie Written While Lying on my Back   151
Upon Revisiting the University of Tennessee   155
I'm Supposed   157
underman   158
City of Brush Fires   160
A Basement Studio   161

Author's Note

The poems in this volume come from an earlier period in Knoxville. Most of them were written then, and the few that were written later were naturally a part of this group. The three books were originally published separately by Rich Mountain Bound, but I always viewed them as a trilogy connected in time and setting and theme. Iris Press publishes them here for the first time together and under this title.

The earlier period I speak of was when I returned to Knoxville in the spring of 1981 after what I call my 'hermit year' in relative seclusion in the Smoky Mountains. When I left the mountains in early '81 I first traveled out west and lived and worked in the state of Washington for a few months before going south to San Francisco. There I stayed for about a month and met a number of writers and artists including some of the Beat writers and their younger contemporaries. By late May I hitchhiked back to Knoxville and started over with the city. It was a wild time of awakening for Knoxville, and of a new self-determination coming into the larger light of a world's fair exhibition soon to take place downtown. In many ways because of this cultural phenomenon, but also in coincidental confluence with it, a series of other cultural and artistic forces were at play that would alter the city's long traditions of art and music and literature.

There are far too many significant details of that time to list here: the many artists, the bands, the exhibition spaces, the incredible number of exhibitions and performances, the skits and plays and performance art, the street art, the Alley des Refusés, the publications, the poetry readings, the manifestoes, the astounding music that was being made everywhere, all the new faces and talents converging on the scene, the many tribes coming together, and all those who were returning to town bringing new energy and ideas from abroad, the new ground being broken, the city politics trying to employ it and then just keep a handle or lid on it all, the new world view and city identity, the recognition of Knoxville's own history and re-connection with its traditions and central figures and movements, the new connections being made to New York and Chicago and Los Angeles and San Francisco and Europe, a changing of the guard in old hard Knoxville.

And from it came the first stirrings of a revival and revitalization of downtown. The Old City itself was born during this time. The latent world's fair site was unwrapped with the reopening of the seven houses that became known as the Artists Colony. This was followed with the opening of the Candy Factory and then the creation of the Knoxville Museum of Art. Long before the decade was over Knoxville would have a new geographical continuum of creative spirit stretched across its center, from UT and the Fort Sanders community through the world's fair site to downtown and into the Old City. It wasn't propped up by any single entity such as the university or the city government, or by any singular event like the world's fair exhibition, but was a legitimate outgrowth of the unfolding culture spawned and held together by a number of entities and events and natural collusion within the city.

For those who were here, it's easy to see the significance of this period. For those who were actively involved, there's always a feeling that the importance of this time has gone relatively unrecognized, often misunderstood, and only marginally documented. So much of importance that was set in motion then is still in play now, still growing out of the seeds and inspiration of those days. These poems are from there.

—RB Morris
December 2006

The Man Upstairs

Return

I am sitting in an attic in Knoxville
I have come a long ways to here
I have come full circle
I was born on this hill where
    hundreds of men died in battle
I began here and now I am back

I have never lived in this house before
This old grandfather who has become my fort
But I have been on this hill
I was born in a hospital
    built upon the battlefield

I am contented here
I have returned from the coasts
    from the roads and people
I have had my hejira and I dreamed
    of being here of coming back
I have looked to the east
    and I have looked to the west
I have asked what I did not know
    and I have learned much
And now I am empty
I am empty and contented
    and I have wandered home

What will you do? I ask myself

Pretending to have a plan, I say
First we must rearrange all these buildings
    and flush the river clean
Reshape the clouds

>   and put back the neighborhood
> Then we must sleep
>
> When we wake
> We will walk down these streets
> We will eat and drink
> We will talk to those we meet
>   and see who they are
> We will return to here

Sleep

One of the great sleeps
is the end of the road sleep
Not death metaphorically
but sleep
A long journey's sleep
The sleep of one come home
Surprised by dawn
and the world still turning
Eyes unexpectedly opening
on the dream

To be at rest
The soul slowly
breathing back
gathering all
the many dancing wheels
the feet have flown
Fading now while
the inner wheel winds
The eyes closed
The wild vision contained
multiplying in silence

It is enough to wake
without ambition or cause
or clockwise voice
and come into this dream
there on the stairs
where you slept
where you saw yourself

somewhere before
and now
before atoms congeal

You saw yourself
a ghost
at rest
where no hand
can lay on

You saw at once
the morning
the journey gone
guitar leaning
in a corner
where echoes ebb
and blur the worlds

I Am Back
did you think
I would remain abroad
indefinitely
for the rest of your life
did you think
life

I am back
did you imagine
me dozing
you looking over
studying closely
the closed eyes
the slow breathing
your mind dreaming
my dreams
that's exactly
what's happening

I am back
did you expect
me to remain aloof
forever
like the old man
dozing in the feather
bed upstairs
the one
we have to shush about
down here
downstairs where all
the puzzles are stacked
and the fireplace is smoking
(better throw another book on)

the old man is waking
(there'll be hell to pay)
his rickety old bones
on the creaking stairs
he's come down to shake
his dreamy head out
and crack a voice

The Attic

The attic is a place of ghosts
forgotten works
a clutter of souls
the high machinery of mind
at watch over household

A spirit forge aflame
above a fireproof floor
An iceland wasteland
tundra asleep

Who goes there?
Who could be called by name?
Who will come to inspect?

A place for dawdlers
curious children
those looking
for something lost
a certificate of birth
never found

But there you are in air
the still undisturbed
dust of the dead
the lost stairway
forgotten floor

THERE WAS A FIRE in the 40's
the garret ablaze
attic windows breathing flame
the beams still charred
few walls stand
makeshift means serving
propped doors stretched canvases
cardboard and curtains
the occasional skeleton of studs
rooms of sorts
some locked off
a place to work
crash
kill time
add to the mumbling whispers
left behind
the unfinished sentence
strewn across old boards
window shades seashells
broken ironworks
a rocking horse
useless plumbing
plaster rolled canvas
papers sculptures
plastic jugs canning jars
cartons boxes books
pushed stacks piled
against discarded articles
picked over and replaced
by artists and others
who sought poorer quarters
inner sanctums
solitude
on margins

sometimes students
those of flesh
and spirit
shedding skin

A Short Sculpture of Tiné

He has his back to you
One elbow a vice the other a wheel
He hits another lick
And sets the chisel down
His face turning
Old steely-eyed but gentle
Michael Tiné
Wanting nothing
A little space
Looking to you
Like a dogfaced marine
And tattoos
After years
The hair and beard long
And working all along
Will pause now
Surrounded by wood and stone
And rack of tools
To turn Beethoven down
And say hello

You first hear him
On the lower floors
The glass front door
Shutting itself
In heavy afternoon
The heavy enough steps
To follow early
Coming on keeping up
'Til finally the attic
Door creaks and the
Last fourteen steps

Lofted up on a landing
Shaking under sudden thud
Of block of wood
A tree stump or chunk of
Marble from the quarry
And the rattlin' of the chains
Old ghost Tiné gathering up the links
To hang on the door
He switches on classical
Preferring no words
So the mind can speak
Freed by deed of work
To float open upon the day
Chipping away stone into night
Grooving wood into
Thoughts circling wild

Always glad to see you
He sips coke from a can
An empty half pint in the trash
The last thing he says
Swinging back is
I'm gonna try'n
Knock this thing out

You Must Bear Water into heaven
It doesn't spring here
You must bear it back out
in your body
You may have stayed the tide
the long night's dreaming
but now to float downstream
the many flowing steps
suddenly exposed to tenants
if a room is open
a resident arriving
or departing the oaken doors
and on down to the ground floor
and out the side door
to more steps
and the hill sloping off
the little shortcut dog path
then jump from the limestone wall
to the sidewalk to the corner
crossing over
to the University Club
hotel and bar with lobby
and backdoor near a bathroom
entering easy unnoticed
to brush teeth wash face
look in mirror sit in stall
read the same small tracts
relieving yourself of all
the night's waste
before leaving discreetly
back into the open day

Fort Sanders

Look! Here's the old neighborhood
of my second childhood
Even then I was dreaming
my days and singing my nights
and talking in my sleep
Even then I sat on old walls
in nostalgic airs of reverie
my body like a tree
rooted in the hillside
Even then I was climbing stairs
to knock on doors
where voices called to me
as I wandered absently
down alleys and lanes
reading the stone walkways
like pages folded out
and fastened to the earth

It is place that founds me
It is hill and river
It is the water under the bridge
The grass that's greener
It is the view of the mountains beyond
and the memory of the sea

WHEN I WAS HERE before
I was another man
I looked different
had another name
People saw me
in a gang or on a stage

Let me explain
I was a soldier then
I either died or escaped
Both the same perhaps
for now I'm changed

I return as a ghost
stalking the old grounds
hardly concerned now
with the latest flurry
of warm breezes
blowing by the hill

It is the secret places
that interest me
The stone wall
where I might stop to rest
The hidden paths
The alleys lined with trees
where birds come to speak
I sit on abandoned steps
of a house no longer there
I lay back against a tree
and listen to sparrows
in a yard where children
haven't played for generations
I might be an old sage in waiting

found out by only those who seek
Invisible to most if seen at all
seen as a ghost or perhaps
an old man, a wino, some dog

And what do I become next?
The ghost of a ghost?
A stone in the hill?
An old tree at the curve
of the trail?
A forgotten house?

WE ARE ALL GHOSTS
are we not?
Spinning a little time
'til timelessness
comes blows the web apart

This house is a ghost
built upon a fort
has haunted itself this century
a bold Victorian apparition
of turrets and balconies
wrapped wide with porches
floors at many levels
cored through from subterranean
cave cellar to airy ethereal attic
with staircases broad
and sweeping in the middle
dark and narrow at the extremes

These streets are shiny ghosts
long and loping
up hill and down
cornered and curled
crossing on grid
running the ridge
A sideways guillotine
for stray dogs
and cats
where feet pass
and avenues open on clouds
A network of wires and poles
where mockingbirds
hold court

The hill itself a ghost
grown long with trees and homes
ribboned round by the river
A birthday present
I can never seem to unwrap

The river too
a ghost of the great circle
No beginning no end
You can't put your foot in
the same place once
the poet said

All ghosts
even these words
a disembodied voice
lost upon air
a hat with no head
blown down the street
searching for a place to rest
some man upstairs
some attic in which to reside
to come alive
and give meaning

WHERE ARE YOU NOW all atom'd up and some body?
The world done come tapped you on the tummy
and made you up some one
What do you do to do time?
Who are you alive?

Free Soup

(for K. Freeman)

Searching out high rooms
Sniffin' long in my high snooze
Talkin' it up with my higher self
I come walking down Laurel Avenue
Looking for free soup

I seen the signs
Let the hungry feed the blind
And climb these old stairs
To some kitchen in the air
Where gather the good people
'Round bowls of split pea noodles
All smilin' and spoonin'
And talkin' and singin'
Playin' music and dancin'
And walls a-hangin'
With pictures and paintin's
And homemade movies flickerin'
In the evening

I said, a ghost toast to angels!
I said, all roads lead to somewhere
And here I am
Said, I follow the tender lamb
Learnt the lamb in the slam
Learnt the lamb and the peacock fan
The underhand and the white tan
And this here
The promised land

I said, all roads lead to here
And this road come through
Fog on the mountain and fog on the river too
You can climb out your window
'Cause this road come through

Through the mud slopped iron shovel grave
Through the hard times the slave days
Through the hard knox nexus of nights
Through the city limits of lost river city
The Bermuda Triangle of the Appalachians!
Fog on the mountain and fog on the river too
Little boy blue go blow your noodle
I said, the sheep's in the bed
And the cow's with the poodle
And the mayor's gone to the wedding

I said, forget about money
Today's a rich day to kick
Change your plans for the evening
Don't play games with art
Don't play smart
I said, let the pop stars P O P
In their LA New York night
Stay here in the light and blow your own world
Blow all the old angels home to roost
And watch that high road come through
And somebody I said somebody
Keep making that free soup

THERE ARE NO LIGHTS tonight looking north
Where is Sharp's Gap?
Where are the radio towers?
It is dark and still
as if no one was there
But we know they are

Maybe there's a storm coming up
The temperature has dropped
Maybe I'm drunk
or just delirious this day
Are we climbing again?
Did I fall back there
on Cumberland?

In the night I heard a voice
Hell is no language
In heaven there is singing
I rested there
arms over the historic marker
attempting to hold paper
to the iron relief of the plaque
breaking my sword through
to the declivity
beneath description

The Assault Upon Fort Sanders

Four brigades of infantry, Gen. James Longstreet's First Corps, emerging from the declivity to the north, made a bayonet charge upon the Federal Fort Sanders at this point, at dawn, Nov. 29, 1863. They were stopped with heavy casualties by a deep ditch and by raking cannon fire. This climaxed Longstreet's siege of Knoxville.

Are you a student?
the old lady asked
I was asleep
passed out against the plaque
forehead imprinting history
The wind had picked up
I looked up
I am not
I
a student
dear lady
I am
holding this
hill

COUNT the stairs
beneath a bare bulb
ascending into darkness
like stars
like nothing
ever witnessed
waiting forever
to fall
you must rise
to occasion
this
eternity
never ends
never begins
no stations
along the way
and the way
is a step

(PARK) (BANK) (12:12) (62°)

Courting insomnia now these hours
Impossible lover to wake
Watching out the window
The bank clock
Holding fast some moment's passing
Towering the air of midnight

Time and temperature
A place of securities?

Inside a universe
A milky swirling pathway
To a blue green stone rolling away
Down cloudy arcs of light
A continent curled back
From froth and humped forth
A mountain a river a town
A hill a neighborhood a house
Three flights up an attic
Window looking out

Yes, we are full of Time
Our hands uplifted in Time
Our minds worn of it
Our hearts absurdly crying for more
Insane once you know it is
Timelessness the soul sings for

Time is everywhere
Choose your point of view

From my window up above
I see the heaps of Babylon
    and hear her radio stations
I watch Helen and Alexandria burn
       hear the faraway clash of shields
     like the clinking of cocktails
      toasting the debris of broken seesaws
     and Phoenician sails blowing by
half burned on the breeze

I breathe in and nap like God
   While the big toe of a Cherokee
    plucks away at bottom lands
I dream good hands in the good river

But he is washed over
Gone like the shadow
      of a june bug
    tied to a string
  dragging away the wigwam day
      into night after night

Some widow maker come
Rattlin' his corpse upon a horse
Some Davy Crockett looking for an Alamo
A fast mare to ride out the fire
A hoary shout whose echo hurts worse
A refrain of unending chorus
     calling us to the broken stars
       if not some manger

From my window up above
I see dawn erupt
I see sharpshooters jogging

       hills of their own making
          hoping for a kill at the clearing
A parody of radios and gym clothes
     dodging bullets and stragglers
      honing a sword in their memory
From my window up above
I see distant sentries
I see battle lines holding
General Longstreet pacing
        the air of stale tobacco
         and indecision

The old war horse
     finally crossing Third Creek
A gray ghost dawn
A white beard of fresh snow
      soon to flow red
           into the hill
        into the river
       held open

And now I see
The hackberry and elm, the maples
    even mulberry and magnolia
Huge oaks that bespeak centuries
But old photos belie such heritage
Tis the blood of the fallen brave
    that sends them so high
       in yet such early age
Was this battlefield not cleared of every tree?
Aye, cleared of every man
A tortured grass dug through
               November rains
        its ditch of death

I can't talk for the blood!
I can't live the life!
I can't love the mouth!
I can't hold what
      was written on my palm!
Disguised I have come home
      with eyes and tongue

Am I to shame for waking up?
Should I not share this cup
      with my sleeping comrades?
Or honor the stillness
      where they lie dreaming?

Fugitive Heart

I am a fugitive poet in my own skin
I have fled myself, my homeland, my kin
Come again unto faces older who knew me
Could not hold me, nor I them
From these lofty ridges we held
We lost and have bartered down our belongings
To the essentials of a private war
From hill to sea, highway to hearth
In search of what was before, shall be now
And never more, O fugitive heart

Paradise

Don't you realize this is Paradise?
This is now
Where it all began
It's true the axis has shifted so often
It's hard to see or believe your eyes
We are bewildered in Time
But consider this, we do know
    that yonder smoky mountains
  are among the very oldest
      in the world
The original red volcanoes
    now forty shades of green
           have seen the sea curl
                  its long arm
       around the steaming
          ground and crack
       and cough up
                  life

Here on this hill
It all began
A garden
And still more wild flowers
       than anywhere on earth
Unless the young Amazon
      has purchased a new
     bouquet or two
   with all her free
        greenhouse time

            The original poem lies
          here in the rise and fall
        flow of East Tennessee

A water closet kept secret
Where God crawled up
                    and took seed
It is the Mother Mountains
    whose breasts we hold in view
A blue ridge to the common eye

There from the corners of the Devil's Cradle
        a split tongue rolled down
                    spewed forth and flowed
            with all its many mouths to feed
                carrying the seed
            into the great circle
The French Broad spreading beneath
            The Holston
        begetting the One
                    the Tennessee

Here near the river
        between two streams
Time stood still long enough
        to swallow its tail
    and rear its head
                inside a dream

This hill is the center of the world
Ask Black Elk
Why do you think it did not fall?
Why do you think it is now so ignored?
Or treated like a whore?

Used for whatever's handy
Burned down paved over
Abused by the elders, these latecomers
Unknowing children grown old
                              with indifference

Their poetry is bad
It lies upon the land
like a poison vine
choking the flow
blocking the line
It infests with time
the slumber of angels
stealing dreams
turning the body over
against itself
If it has its way
the house will not stand

They number the streets
They number the creeks
They have no loving touch
Nor imagination much
They would call the river a lake
A four letter word
Something they made
They would change Gay Street
      to Commerce
It's all for appearance

Who decides such details?
Who names the animals?
Your Tigris and Euphrates
You call Second and Third

What happens if you get turned around?
Going upstairs or down?
You may drown from bad directions
Suffer us not your lack of true possession

Am I not your poet?
I was born to name you
I have returned now to claim you

The long street you call 17th
Should be named for the fool
Who laid siege and assault there
Longstreet

Your flowing creeks
That you made into sewers
Killing the healing waters
The very lifeblood of your body
You no longer have the right
To call your own
In the order you found them
They should be known as

Fountain Creek
Home Creek
Hill Creek

The river by any other name
Would smell the same
Once you poison its waters
But why rob it further dignity
With some second rate misnomer?
Even your second rate designs
Would be served much better

By telling the world
Through your fair city
Flows the Tennessee River

And though Knoxville is the name
By which you will be called to supper
Tanasee, Tennessee of the Cherokee
Would serve you much better

Just do remember
The river is a river
It was here before you came
It will be here long after
You and all the dams
Are gone again

Crow-Morris Man

Crow-Morris Man died out
Some billion years ago
Long before Cro-Magnon Man
But then
What flies around
Flutters back again

CROWS IN THE CITY

You see them occasionally
A lone scout eyeing dumpsters
From a dead mimosa
Or a murder of them flapping
Back to the suburbs with news
Of conquest or gossip
The black raiders
Country smart and come to town
To swindle trade steal
Whatever's there for bounty

They slip through from
Surrounding hills and fields
Some arrive by interstate
Where the spoils of commerce
Leave them road kill
The bare locusts and saplings
Too driven or exposed
For any enemy or those who
Can't abide the old boys

They were here on a frosty morn
In their great coats
Waiting for Longstreet's blunder
Not caring the cold or the color
Knowing black would outlast
Blue or gray

Local Man

Don't you see?
I can't be Christian
      even though I love Christ
Or Buddha
      though I may laugh
    'til my eyes slant with tears
I can't even be Existential
      even though I am

I can't be Beat
   even though I'm beat
or Dada
   even though I'm nothing

I can't even be literary
Even though I lay down in the sound
That's been laid down
Even though I sleep with history
And fashion my thoughts to fit a muse
      who lives in my vicinity

I can't be Thomas Wolfe
      or James Rufus Agee
even though I may search my past
      as if it were my face
        in the mirror
of some home away from home

even though I may value life
      above art
should one not be one

I may throw stones
            and kick leaves about
        and talk of my father's
          pure strand of pearls
            handed down
     through my mother's lips
             to an unfound door
But no more for emulation
                than locale

"The Man Who Lives Here Is Loony"

(for J. Agee)

He was living in Brooklyn at the time
In the garret of some house
On Saint James Place
Where he kept a goat
And someone wrote it on the door

He was used to that by then
And kept on working through the night
As he always did

After he died
They published his last book
And gave him a Pulitzer Prize
Then they put his first one out again
Called it an American classic

He Likes to Talk about angels
He likes to call all people angels
He wants to see the angel in everyone
And of course he does
He may say there are wings
Attached to all of us
You just have to see them
He's very adamant about this
Often alluding to holy scripture
And other poets when admonishing
The apathy around him
He likes to start at the beginning
And work away into his altruism
He adores the letter *A*

The Man Upstairs

I must be the man upstairs
The one with the fly in his ear
I must be the old buzzer
Up there

I must be the one who finds me dead

When you think I'm out of my head
I'm asleep

I must sleep

Of course you can stop anywhere
And hear echoes
Hear whatever you want to hear
Did you hear that?
Do you wish to stop here?
I don't suppose there's any hurry
Are you waiting for someone?
Do you want to go on alone?
Listen that singing
I'll be right back

The stairs lead to the inner ear
Where he dozes in a chair
An open hand
The radio half off the station

I saw him sleeping there
Partially covered in a blanket

I hadn't noticed
There is a door
And more steps ascending
Disappearing behind him
In the dark

I hear him up there
He wakes me up singing
I'm sure he sees me
He knows I'm coming to
And sings softer
And softer
Just a hum
And sometimes
I can almost remember
Remember the words
Then he's laughing
Moments later
When I doze off again
I realize
I'll never quiet him
Unless I wake up
I'm beginning to understand
I think
I know what kind of music
He likes
I hear him having conversations
In his sleep
Trying to convince someone
I heard him on the stairs
Going on for hours
Sometimes I can't tell
I don't know
If it's him or me

That's sleeping
Sometimes I think
He never sleeps
Only me
Asleep

When God Dozes

Ole Moon was turned on his head
Agape agog a ghost again

I was standing at the top of the stairs
It was cold as hell

There were no snakes in Eden now
Where was Eden?

And God? God was asleep

Shivering shaking wondering how deep
Should I wake?

No! said God who only dozes
And hears all prayers and poesies

Sleep child, sleep 'til dawn
For soon, soon we rise and move on

Me too! said Ole Moon

Nails

It's like Corso said
The nails went through
The man to God
And see how he's caught?
Can this be talked?
It's like my brother said
God is a refuge
In a warehouse in the sky
And how can he fly
If we hold him?
Behold him
The man
Driving home
His steel vision
Trying to fasten down
The unseeable breeze
Creating storms to no avail
And wasn't Jesus a carpenter
Who knew the price of nails?

the tallest wall
in the world
is a word

Life

Life is a lesson in faith
I am talking about gravity
Life is a stone stacked against another
I am speaking of spirituality
Life flows and is a river of language
I am referring to biology
Life is a way to come
I am reciting poetry

We will not be able to follow
And then we will meet

Life is a stick in the mud
I am alluding to art
Life is an old hat passed
Down the generations
And finally given away
I am talking about religion

The Ice Storm of '81

When the winter had come
And the winds had blown
Every map every picture every poem
Off the wall
Tearing old plastic
From staples and nails
Covering holes
That once held windows
When the icicles hung
From my unshaved face
And mustache
And all my clothes and blankets
And further efforts
Could not dispel the chill
From my bones

I carried myself and some
Few belongings
Into Eric's studio
Where were windows
And heater and couch
Whereon I lay
For one cold week
With clenched teeth
On Clinch Avenue
Frozen in a crystal dew
Like a still life
Of Knoxville

This Space Heater
Appears to have been born
Of the Middle Ages
Like some very early rocket
Bringing itself to near lift-off
Every half minute
But always subsiding back
To the cold fact
Of being before its time

A Girl Came Upstairs

1

A girl
came upstairs
I was busy
telling the world
about my dead
friend
she wanted
to talk
about building
a cabin

2

I suppose I knew she was married
though she never said
and wore no ring
when she invited me
to join her poetry group
one evening
I came down from my haunts
a little early
before others arrived
only her husband
whom one would never suspect
except he brought her supper
the basic burger
not even any cheese
I didn't think
he was her husband

I didn't think
I stared at her the whole time
people read their poems
she was the only poem
I longed to have on my tongue

I didn't realize
how desperate I was
'til then
how long it had been
since I had felt affection
from a woman

3

So he left her the pillow
but not the pillow slip

only this
and a blanket

She smiled out the window
at the rain

He would like to see me
go home

She said turning
to look at me

across the empty room
no couch

to rest her hand upon
He never wants to see me

again she said
Do you believe that?

4

I long for the moments
when everything is let down

like your thoughts
your clothes

this pose of propriety
I want something golden

to happen in a kiss
something wet and fast

5

happy hour
"I know I'll get published!"
"yes but will you get kissed!?"
"get kissed!?"
"yes!"
"by the people who read my book!?"
"no on the mouth!"
"on the mountain!?"
"on the mouth!"

6

A hidden patio
in back under the magnolia
beyond where the buildings
close and rise
a narrow slate stone
walkway between
leading to
a back stairway
behind a coke machine
at top inside
a utility closet
then her room
number 7
I have stood at that door
looked through the vent slants
to the shadows of her floor
seen them darken
as her sock feet shuffled
to my knock
she let me take showers
she liked to peek
around the curtain
the window on the far wall
faced the landlord's apartment
she told me once she saw him
walking around naked over there
I was sure the bastard
was aware and orchestrated this
she could easily have lived
rent free
he was hell to deal with
once he suspected

something was going on
between us

7

I fancied myself in love with her
I fashioned my love like the decline of Rome
She was much like a third world country
Finally gaining some independence
Anxious to walk tall among the young barbarians
Not at all eager to be a satellite to any sun
We danced at a distance
I changed clothes often
I made sure she saw me on the balcony
When I tossed the fiddle to the void

8

Downstairs she's beating on the ceiling
with a flaming broom
with the skull of a burning woman
I know that code (the pipes glow)
They take me and wash me
in a stone cave
her multi-colored eyes everywhere
When I awake she's here in the room
I lose her in a circling crowd of faces
The music is so loud and keeps stopping
She's in the corner
her hair hung from a rafter
a demon's grin on her mouth
Then she's beside me whispering
softly gently next to me
her eyes closed in benevolent dream

I see her breasts beneath her gown
She wants this
looking the other way nudging closer
She asks me to come downstairs with her
She asks me again with her eyes
She asks me again
I hear the birds singing outside
My eyes fly
She is gone

Now As the Ancient Night

Now as the ancient night spreads new
There is a constellation comes into view

It is of course
Lonely and very distant
A balance
You may much admire
In light of your needs
Just a glimpse now and then
Though seldom here and now
Just something to draw upon
Like thoughts of death

And think how far
The tear will fall
Before the idea is done
Like being caught in a warm rain
This very Spring
Standing and gazing
Not thinking
Falling

Abandoned on a stairway
Tapping the dust in your cuff

And wonder what it is
What it is
Think it a cello
Or some very old fiddle
Even a blue guitar
But never just the dark
Where the air is full
And you go play

Song For A Changing Season

The birds like bells this dawn
Turning back the world
Into a song
They roll away the fog

Through my window a sky
Hangs tilted
And somehow connected
To some sea below

Not gulls but robins singing
No palms but magnolias
Blossoming down on
This soaring clear morn

Time lost in a crystal
No dismal clock
Nor cloud to mark
This sweet dismissal

Yesterday so dark
Would mock
My head bowed
My heaven's door

And bottoms up
Some ocean floor
To blot
This newest gown

But he is away back there
On his battlefield
A waif waylaid though wafting still
O're broken shields

And here he cannot touch
Cannot stir such fuss
Nor drum out this tenderest
Lull of newfound emptiness

Then let the sky fill up
With blue and cup this day
And pour me off a shiny token
These windows now so open

EVICTION

In the most sublime moment they enter
The ghost stargazing at noon

Eviction comes in dark blue suits
Boasting badges tacking notice
Knowing full well
Who pays them for what
The unspoken plot

The fire marshals found an open door
Always exactly what they're looking for
No warrant needed
They emerge in private air
The hollow hand of the long arm
Behind them the teeth uptown
The fractured judicial jawbone

In the name of celebration
Heaven sponsors death
Those resisting separation
Will be joined with nothing

The face in the cloud turns away

Lucifer has been asked to leave
For the sake of unanimity
The angels all agree
The landlords acquiesce
Adam has his walking papers
The god walking blues
A gone daddy
Exodus stage west

The Man Upstairs

I must be the man upstairs
The one I heard about
The one in the dream
At the top of the stairs
Like an odd crow in a magnolia
Like a man
With his head in a cloud
Looking over the city
Sleeping in

the door that was always open
now is locked
if you don't have a key you have to knock

There is a war in Fort Sanders
There are skirmishes in doorways
There are spies in driveways
Where they put their signs
Where they put their fear
In the hearts of young dumb students
Who don't even know
There is a war
They have stormed the garret
They have condemned the attic
They would torch this Church
This Home
This Fort
Bring this old Grandfather down
But they can't have this holy ground
Go tell the man uptown
Beware
Of the man upstairs

don't indulge your dreams
I heard in a dream
good way to let the man downstairs in

I don't forget the mote and the beam
But this iniquity I don't ignore
I'd be no more than another statue lost
Among the stone heads in this quarry
I say if you must choose
Then go with Beauty
But what are their dreams?
Dumb show and Greed
Weigh them out
On a scale of Time
Nothing do they satisfy
Hold them up
To Timelessness
Do you see an empty hand?
Now who is Blind?
Who has Vision?
Time is a prison
From which the Spirit flies
Who will take Possession?

though you guard the heart
the body is a house
you must be prepared to leave

The upper rooms are filled with dust
Just a high and lonely tomb
Where once I chased the ghost
Where my days are numbered
Where my nights are numb
Break open the roof beams!

I want my wings
Let down the ladder
These chains are fallen
Hold forth and fly this sunken floor!
We have a volunteer

there was an article in the paper
about a local man having to live
in a burned out attic with no windows

I was happy here
The man upstairs
Could sit and think
Go out for a drink
Come back and sleep
Over my city

Behind Enemy Lines

The lines are drawn
They are fine with me

The day the night
The long mystery

Is it I who decides
Which way these stairfalls rise?

I climb the walls
Only to pass the time

Only to rest on the other side

Littoral Zone

My cousin Bobby is windsurfing
The sun is going down shimmering
on the Ashley River
The bracky tide coming in
Lucinda has placed a shark's tooth
on the arm that writes
and hung a little crab's leg off my ear
The gulls are wafting about like distant relatives
My ass on the shelly sand
and my hairy feet in the surf

—Charleston travel journal
Summer '83

CHINA WAITS by tiny rivers for the dragonfly's return. Glaciers the size of a finger. Written on sand, like Breton trailing Picabia with an eraser. Along those shores, down by the banks, the mudflats and rocks, out to the tidal plain where fiddler crabs dance and turtles race and shrikes sweep off the sky. Where memory lives in the wind and surf or is buried at sea. Earth, air and water, and none claims total dominion. Ebb and surge. Mathematics drowned in the moon. A lunule littoral wonky and gibbous in the limned niello. A bottom line tying the world in a sailor's knot. An intricate global network. Old proving ground where life steps forth.

VERTICAL HORIZONS. Vitreous mirage backed by steel. Strange mosaic tessellating twixt endless tributaries of pavement flushed under wires by walls, doorways, windows, telephone poles, purling down alleys eddying out into pools of parking lots. A land of slaves, obsessions, commerce. Forgotten works where wellsprings protrude. A raveled mesh of architectures, the restacked matchsticks. Morphoses unremembered. Blocks of boxed-up buildings. A maze. Walls waylaid in time, moored by gravity. Ruin upon ruin purloined of history's leaky pocket, whose draggled skirts have mounted yet another curb, serried forth and ricocheting off the moment hying on toward death's agog lophophore. Statue entering a niche. Jonah on another shore.

Gulls turning into pigeons
Off the sloping banks of the interstate
Watching life flow by
Not knowing when we go with it
Not knowing how it works for sure
Pigeons turning into gulls
My mother calling me
The fiddler crab edging back to the hole
Somewhere in the muck and flow
And sand breaking up
A tide moves like God's hands of a clock
Slow enough to where some say
It doesn't move at all, prove it
And you say too
And set about upon the waters

WHEN THE PIGEONS LIFT UP one more time
To circle the dusty trees over Jefferson Street
Pulled by some unseen force to loop the distance
Of roofs and flutter back like an old film
Played through again

Then there is a city
Somehow lifted
In the eye
In the waking heart

So it begins in varied sequence
To unfold and solidify surrounding hills
Still holding now familiar contours
Recognized from cars careening by
Stretching out the edge of grids
Souls mapped over in a tableau of webs

Who is it walks out these streets?
Emerging from side roads and leafed alleys
Appearing upright at intersections
Crossing over passing other bodies lost and lingering
Waiting for who knows what in this play of the heart?
A walker embodying some purpose it would seem
Held back by lack of wings or greater vehicle
Leaning toward some hill
One leg crossing the other
One step one street at a time
Traversed and put behind
In immediate walking karma
The only symmetry made known to a naked eye
All else just gusting theology
A young philosopher's contention
An art student's dream

Who passes these outposts?
Not yet bearing some tattered insignia
Of yore and by no sign connected
To the market's mightily fueled wheel
No smell of scorch from the hallowed fires
Of souls possessed?
What left to the eyes of nature
After science has chewed on it awhile?
Pushing through with only two feet
A small engine of the heart
And where but in this world somewhere?
And there you too, good follower
There you too

Walk, for we have come to this
Stood tall and looking about
Braced by sky and memory of the sea
Erected now on a ladder of genes
We surpass ourselves with no direction
Step forth and stretch the eyes of nature
For the heart is not satisfied
Cranky and dancing too
But the muscles of the beast
Still know the whip is nigh
So, where ends the feeble mind?
Does it even speak?
Walk and give rhythm to the voice
Walk and give rise to the world
We were told of a thinking creature
A third eye or some benevolent heart

Let us follow then

We find him early already present
There where the morning comes beating
Like a drum on the banks of the river
A song lifting up
Rising from the depths
Echoing even yet as we
Draw near the edge

Poets I Have Followed Around

We stand on the other side of the door
We try for the knowing knock

Through the keyhole he goes to the window
We see him hang by his hands above the city

Outside we wait for a sign
We hear the typewriter cough

We go home together get drunk
Talk 'til we find something to argue about

We follow him to where he passes out in the garden
We see the golden eternity through his eyelids

We dangle our feet over the old abyss
Pointing south into chiaroscuro

We translate moans in the dark
Change our names and pluck an eye out

We study mystics who break our feet
We walk out the backdoor with gypsies

We brave the river and sleep under ancient pines
We dream ourselves dreaming ourselves

At dawn we embark on fossil hunts
Eat herbs turn into dinosaurs with Chinese eyes

We leave the mountain trail for bird paths
Laughing with old hermits under cliffs

We speak with dolphins
Read hieroglyphs in the sand

We wander through an Araby of our own making
We join the foreign legion

We become Greek go home
We dive off the bridge until marriage

We hide in a treehouse then a cave
We devise an old song to hang on the taxman

We attempt to fly and almost pull it off
Perfecting a scoff for the sake of skyscrapers

We meet the holy ghost on the street
Become tongue-tied talk too much

We ask her if she will take tea or wine
She writes on the wall with her eyes

We see the folly of weathervanes
And crow it from every barn

We take off our shoes and socks
And dance on our heads for days

We smoke a peace pipe with the world
Go back to sleep

We follow a child through a house
Recalling our other lives

We read giant books of arcane verse
Screaming out the window at the ice cream man

He smiles inside a dreamsicle
We build an altar to the sun

We sleepwalk through a world's fair
Wake up at the gates of the city

Upon Meeting Gregory Corso on the Steps of The St. Francis of Assisi Catholic Church in San Francisco

>*Are you Gregory Corso,* said I
>*I am,* said he
>And there we sat
>At the feet of Francis of Assisi

ON THE BUS we go, all of us who go. And we are diverse, a simultaneity in different mediums, the young and the old and the temporarily lost between. A raucous titanic leaking out on the morning. Embarrassed businessmen and tawdry denizens in whorled locutions. The bag ladies hold forth, ankles taped for the fray. They solidify as the bus surges and settle into heaps on hard seats beneath dumb advertising. Other more perfumed simpáticos timidly wage the simplest of niceties through the ages, offering up amelioratives to their familiars. Some are completely still, caged in tatters and silence, balustrading from homes and hospitals where they find no rest. I see their eyes in the window reflection.

Outside, the children of fates, scattered fold standing around where so many have stood, walking out the beaten paths, the long and broken wheel of faces. A museum of curios outcropped in rock and kudzu. The construction crew. A crumbling of time and sound. Others beside the road waiting for the greater vehicle, gawking inward.

The bus driver is Buddha. He is even happy. Mother to all the black eyes and empty bottles. He is in control. I am in and out, on and off. Art is not the greater vehicle, but it's good for the distance. I advise all students of poetry to ride the bus.

City

1

I have traveled extensively in this city. Beginning at her limits I have sup't the tit of the milky way and lost my way home. Only to wake in the warm folds of her hills, and watch her grow old, my leg bent to her crossroads. Turning over the years, laughing an idiot's laugh and crying the tears of reoccurring dreams. Dug in. Excavating that belated future that keeps shifting with the sands and sifting with the silt into the river that split her.

2

There she lies. A few scaly escarpments and jagged protuberances skylining her back like a beleaguered old stegosaurus laid down to die, or maybe just rest awhile before dragging on in time. Catapulting clouds fly past eliciting pale observations from arcane weather charts as humans come and go like a dazed child thumbing through a comic book under a tree. Such is history. The beast groans and turns over opening an eye on the unbelievable dream.

3

Was it all just a cloud that turned into another cloud by end of day, lost over a lost sea like so much floating time never to be told in this old hejira of the soul? O holy city! A bride abandoned at the altar? The groom was late? O chanced rapture! Gone and forgotten like some crazy dream let go in the light of day? Then blow me away! sang the lost tribe of children grown old, and blow down these mountains that held us like babes to their breasts, blow down the great halls of sun and sea and let us rest a sleeping ghost in the breath of God's good tea.

The Acts Man

Anyone living in this city who has eyes has seen him.
I've seen him for as long as I remember. The ghost of
Magnolia, the man with the mirror. Old street character
of endless rumor. Dope dealer, pervert, murderer. Some
say voodoo man, black magic. Some say Cuban, some
say crazy man. Most say a bum anyway

Sinister and tragic
And always with the bike and sign
That ridiculous mobile wigwam contraption
The peephole in the rain another
Roadside attraction

Weird street preacher who don't got no voice
Acts 2:38 or Hell, sign says, take your choice

The Acts Man. Prophet Wilson. Born where the
greyhound bus station now stands. Mother black,
father red. Fellaheen favorite son come home
to the wilderness to minister the civilized barbarians.
Standing astraddle a city corner where the rushing
worlds collide, the hastening tides of humanity
converging. All the mad driven gnashing anonymous
cars merging like ants on an anthill. Traffic horned
as if the very hounds of hell rode shotgun to every
empty destination. An insane circuitous parade that
day after day keeps us separated one from another,
the black the white the man the woman the rich
the poor.

But separated also from ourselves, the other.
Give over, your sign says, give over. We are a bridge
between flesh and spirit. There's more to have if we
want it.

Why look to the sky
The ghost is within

Chained to all those devils you and him. Feed me, fuck
me, blow smoke in my face, I'm thirsty, now praise me
and let me sleep. O deep deep.

Caught we are pacing the gilded cage. Living the life,
humping the age. And who the one that stands apart?
A most visible and vulnerable soul you are. Stranded
it would seem to such talk as this and worse. Strange
man of the holy ghost.

Upon Meeting Prophet Wilson

When I first saw you standing in the grass
Feeding the birds like Saint Francis
Strangely bare of your bike and sign
Your back bent tossing bread
I thought for a moment it wasn't you at all
But some old man, and waited
'Til you turned to make an introduction

The new white January sun coming cleanly
Down settling on your dark glasses
You looked long at me and spoke slowly
Arms folded, old coat loosely adorning

And there was a little kitten came stealing
Past your feet, and I suppose
Thinking you wouldn't mind or see
Pounced on a crumb or two to eat
"Stay out of that" said you with mock wrath
"That's for the birds. Stay away from that."
But added last, "Okay, get you some,
But leave the rest," and then you asked
"What do you know about spiritual things?"
"Well, not enough," I thought fast

There was some caution undisclosed
In the way you spoke and stood apart
Later you would tell me
"No man knows what's in another man's heart."

It was certain you surveyed me
In my censorship of sight

Your one-way shades fixed about
My white hands and hitchhiker's bible
A long awkward frame I felt myself
Too slender to be serious
Restless from one leg to another
Tongue tied and flapping in the breeze
And you said, "Let me ask you this,
Why did you come to see me?"
"Because I've seen you," is all
I could think to say

And following you down the outside steps
Entering eye level to the ground
An old basement floor you asked me to switch
Off a light when you switched another on
And stepping over a dark room I'd tried to
Memorize moments before keeping an eye
On a vague glow around a cluttered corner
Finally coming into your space your domain
A woodstove crackling next to a cot
A comic page laid over a door for a tablecloth
A naked bulb suspended in the subterranean air
And there we sat for hours keeping the fire
Burning beneath the church beneath the world
The people the birds and cats and cars and
Rumors and all mysteries that remain

There I saw your eyes and heard your story

And talk of life and possible life
Of power of the mind and faith
Of blind wanderers in a vast wilderness
And what you'd seen

From visions you had when you were twelve
To men in the last year who
Have tried to kill you

Coffee and raisin bread you offered me
I offered to tell others
What I had learned of you
What was true and not true

"Oh you can't do that" you said
"People will take your words
And beat you with them."
"They don't beat me," I said, "They
beat themselves."
"Well," said you, "If you want to,
You can tell them I'm not crazy.
You can tell them that, maybe."

Song for Atlantic Avenue

The workingmen come walking
They lean across the stone
Huddled up in hats and coats
They take themselves toward home
A journey that each day
Begins anew on Atlantic Avenue

The puddles in the parking lot
Reflecting the sky
As the evening rain lets up
In the glow of twilight
The crack between two worlds
Comes into view on Atlantic Avenue

Darkness falls forever
On broken wheels and dreams
Alley cats and night birds play
In the shadows and machines
A signal from the streetlamp
Breaking through on Atlantic Avenue

Windows in old houses
Glowing rosy in the night
Lost within exhausted sleep
Sheltered in the life
And the stars above twinkle out
Of the blue on Atlantic Avenue

IN A LAZY lost and found afternoon
His younger brother and I discovered him
Years dead now embedded at the edge
Of dirt and concrete
A monument of sorts
A name in stone
A man who came to this city
To attend the university
And lived in this neighborhood
As his brother Jack would later do
Long after he passed
Wandering the same streets
To find where he signed his name
In the sidewalk one fresh day

*Was it Folly? Most likely, or was it Lady's Island?
I was only three maybe four years old. We were
walking by the sea, the waves gently turning and
lapping in slow motion as the film plays back.
My mother was walking with my dad and my aunt
and uncle. She was very beautiful wearing a 50's style
bathing suit. My dad and uncle not long back from
the war. I ran ahead in the bright sun and when I
heard my mother laughing I looked back and saw
she had propped herself on the curved limb of
a large piece of driftwood and was posing like a movie
star. She laughed and we all laughed with her and
walked on by the sea.*

*—Charleston travel journal
Summer '84*

THE LITTLE BOY was so amazed at everything
but mainly the amazing impossible screen where
cowboys rode horses so fast and dust roared up with
the great looming west all around and the cowboy
in the white hat drew his pistol quicker and shot the
man with the mustache who looked mean at her and
he felt alright about that and laughed with his dad
and everyone else when the horse kissed the girl

and he felt close to the people in the theater when
they laughed together but it was kind of hot and
smelly too but then suddenly it wasn't hot at all but
rather cool and there were twinkling lights along
the wall and up in front he thought he saw a man
on stage playing a giant pump organ like his
grandma's only so much grander and all the
sound surrounded him and he heard children

laughing and turned to look in the dark but the
flashing colors of cartoons leaping out made him
hop a little in his seat and his dad was smiling down
sweetly into his eyes but then a question in his squint
that meant do you have to pee but no he said with his
eyes and a shake of his head and was excited again
having never seen such things at the theater before
and looking past his dad down the dark aisle he

saw the faces of the men as they sat in the
flickering light of the screen staring up in awe
and question and then they were laughing and his
dad laughed too and everybody laughed but
when he looked past his dad again he saw children
laughing and one was standing in his seat pointing
to the screen and he looked at his dad who was still
smiling up and not really noticing the people

and what did it mean except yes it is indeed
magical at the theater and things happen here and
we never know how but only that movies are so
special and all the people and the way it changes
and there would be much to talk about later and
ask his father and he was a little perplexed but very
pleased and had many questions about what he
saw and his dad asked him did you enjoy that son

and yes he said he did and his eyes said more and
he wanted to ask much more as they walked outside
and the night had come and the world was changed
from the way it was before and not so crowded now
and they walked along his father much taller
than himself and he saw the big buildings above his
head against the night sky and some had signs and
names and some of these he could say to

himself and his dad held his hand when they
stepped down to cross the street but then let go after
they stepped back up on the sidewalk and walked
along more like friends he thought and made sure
to step quickly enough to keep up but only his dad
knew the way to go which way to turn and though
he looked as far as he could see he still wasn't sure
and it was a mystery the long shadowed streets

and little lanes and sometimes lights flashed out
and people laughed out loud or just as suddenly
it was silent and dark again and this is the city he
said to himself where we live only their street was
a good long walk from here and there were houses
and yards and trees and it was always quiet and
pleasant there and his dad turned down a smaller
street that opened onto the Market Square and he

remembered walking here in the bright light of
afternoon with his mother and aunt in a crowd but
now there were only a few lights and a few people
sitting quietly and his father nodded to them as
they passed and he watched how some stared back
and how they looked like farmers and country
folk like the people they see on Sundays when
his dad drives them out in the country and

suddenly he saw two men to the side of the
Square who were talking very fast and paid no
attention to them as they passed and weren't dressed
like country folks at all but in clothes he had never
seen before and his dad didn't nod but looked straight
ahead and walked on until he turned into an open
door of a smoky room and inside it was warm like the
theater and the faces there were rosy and dark and

it smelled more like sweat and he held his dad's
hand and leaned against him as he stood at the bar
and looked down the room and then talked to a man
and said I'll have a whisky and the man brought him
a glass and his dad drank it down in a swallow like
the medicine his mother gives him that doesn't
taste good and you have to swallow it fast so you
don't taste it but you still do taste it and it makes

you make a face even if you don't want to but she
said it was good for you and then his dad lifted him
up and set him on the bar where he could see down
the room and the faces turned toward him and some
of them smiled and he smiled back and then they
laughed which made him feel shy but his dad
was there with him and he said that's my boy and
they smiled again and went back to talking and he

heard the sounds of all their voices and how some
were louder and stuck out and then others
and all the voices were all one sound and then there
was music mixed in with the voices and then the
music was louder than the voices and he looked to
see where it was coming from and there were lights
lit up along the wall and people sitting at tables
he hadn't seen before and the man who brought

the glass to his dad was dressed differently when
he brought him another glass and there were others
dressed the same in black shirts who walked past
and the lights were turned on down the bar
and people were standing and talking and moving
about and he could see the whole room now and
along the wall were big pictures of faces and it was
all a little much for him to take in and he looked at

his dad who was staring ahead lost in some thought
like he sometimes was when he would ask him
a question and he didn't hear at first but then he
would answer like he had heard all along and so he
waited for him to answer although he hadn't asked
him this time but only looked at him and
saw just past his face a picture on the wall of a huge
dark face with dark eyes looking straight down at

him and beside it he could read *A little too much*
is just enough for me and he wanted to show his dad
how he could say this but he didn't want to brag
because his dad said bragging wasn't good and he
wanted him to think he was smart but he didn't want
him to think he was a bragger so he just hoped his
dad might ask him or see the picture too but his dad
just stared ahead thinking to himself until he turned

and said well let's head on and lifted him back
down and patted his head and took his hand as they
walked outside and when they got to the street
he reached in his coat and took out some candy and
they each took a piece to suck while they walked
and tried not to bite and just let it melt all the way
'til they got to that great wide street that goes over
to the L&N Station and is like a river they always

say that they're crossing over to the other side
and when they get there they wash up out of the
water to where the station stands so big like a
church with its stain glass windows still glowing
in the night as they passed and saw people inside
but when he looked back he saw the glow go out
and watched it grow dark and old like an old man
sighing as it sunk down by the road and faded in

the shadows behind them as they walked on to
the bridge and he looked up at his dad who was
looking ahead and didn't see but suddenly said
listen here comes a train and just then the whistle
blew and they knew it was close and they ran as
fast as they could and when they got to the middle
it was just coming under and he lifted him up so he
could see the big engine passing below and puffing

black smoke and the whistle blew again this time
even louder as it rumbled beneath him like he was
riding the boxcars and the engine pushed on into
the great rail yard and started to slow and disappear
in the dark but suddenly then there were lights
popping on like little dots all over the yard and way
down the valley to another bridge and beyond far
down the way lit up everywhere as far as he could

see a million lights shining and blinking and flashing
like ferris wheels turning and fireworks exploding
in the evening sky and the train blew its whistle one
last time and he had to catch his breath not knowing
what in the world it could be and his dad just laughed as
he sat him back on his feet and said I remember when
you were afraid to let me hold you up when that old
train came through and he laughed again and turned

to walk on across the bridge and he couldn't say
a thing but tried to keep up as he grabbed for his
hand and was afraid to look back but then he did
at the old dark yard where the train had stopped and
cars clanged to a halt but there was only the dark
and the smell of soot and he looked at his dad from
a half step behind and hurried along until they
stepped off the bridge and onto the lane and slowed

down some then and let loose of his hand and he
knew for sure this was their neighborhood and
it was good to be near to his home but there was no
hurry now and they slowed down a little more and
strolled along beneath the streetlamps and when
his dad stepped off into the grass he stepped off into
the grass too and they walked over a ways to a tree
by a big rock and they sat on the rock his dad sitting

first and then he sat up beside him and they didn't
much talk but just looked out past the leaves into the
dark and you could see a few stars and a ridge there
beyond and then they heard a man walking back on
the sidewalk and they saw him pass under the
streetlamp and walk on unaware of them sitting there
and they didn't say a thing until he was gone and
after a while his dad began to hum a little song

and sang a few lines and hummed a little more
and then they were quiet and just sat for a spell
looking out at the night and heard the engine again
when it huffed in the yard and the cars as they shifted
and they shifted too on the rock where they sat
and his dad rested his arm in back of his head and
they continued to sit and kept looking off and *It
was probably here somewhere in here* they heard

a voice say but they couldn't see who for there
wasn't a soul no one at all as they sat looking out
and his dad didn't move but only kept watching out
past the leaves and out past the town and the ridges
beyond and *probably right* he heard a reply obviously
not realizing that they were right there and *well
you'd think there'd be something some outcropping
here* and oh my heart he suddenly knew

that's where we're sitting and there were
two voices there just there in the dark who
were looking for them *well not necessarily you
know a lot has been lost in a hundred years* and
yeah I guess you're right and 10th *came in just over
there* and *of course who's to say if there really
was a rock he might have just dreamed that part
up* and *yeah you never know* and they were sure

to be found now the voices so close to where
he sat with his dad who only ignored them like
the man who was walking and kept looking off
and so he did the same and they said not a word
and moved very little and heard nothing else until
he brought his hand over on top of his head and
held him even closer and after a minute smiled
down and said hey we better go 'fore your mom

starts to worry and he pulled him a little tighter as
if they were cold and gave him a squeeze and then
they stood up and brushed off their pants and went
back to the street and all the way home they both
walked in silence the little boy wondering at what
he had heard and all he had seen and if his father
would tell him just what it all means and did it
make perfect sense or if he should ask

THERE are old sidewalks in the city of rivers. Sidewalks time and weather have made wondrous art of. If wondrous art were enough, they might be kept intact, framed by famous streets. But they'll be replaced with clean slates. Their intricate cracks more beautiful than all Duchamp's broken glass.

The Ragman

I

What's the matter? I asked the Ragman, just to see if he'd talk. I'd seen him making his rounds day to day downtown and back. I figured he'd see me as any man and say just what he thought.
It's you, he said, looking down at his shoes.
I said, No, I mean, I thought there must be some reason you...I mean, for me, I'm just lost around here now. I got it bad for somebody who could care less, you know? I mean, tell me what it is makes a man want a woman *so bad* he'll give up everything he's got?
It's hard to sit at the sidewalk near the curb where strangers walk by so close and above you, and death's a tire squeal away. But heartsickness leaves you stranded, and as misery loves company you sometimes feel joined with people you suspect might be as lost as yourself.
It's a hole, he said.
A hole?
Yeah. You got a hole in you, big as your eyes.
Hey, I know about holes, I said. I got seven in me now, not counting the one I been thinking bout blowing through my brain.
That's when he first looked at me, but didn't say a thing.
What do you mean a hole? I humored him.
He took a last drag off the cigarette, cupping his hand so some of the smoke would go in his nose.
You see that car got stopped on the bridge there yesterday?
What car?
That old car quit running on the bridge and they got all

backed up.
Yeah, I said, I heard something about that. Caused a wreck didn't it, right at rush hour?
Ran out of gas, he said, he was plum empty.
Yeah? So what, I thought.
He dropped the butt between his feet and let slip a perfectly aimed slither of spit past arms and knees to the little mark already dead. For extra measure he raised the front of his shoe and crossed it over dragging the butt back, a thin black smear on the pavement.
Spare a smoke? He asked, almost looking up.
I'm out, I said, showing him the deflated pack, squeezing it in my hand. Smoked my last one. But how can that be? How can I get so bent out of shape over this girl?
She got the power, he said.
The power? How does she have the power?
You gave it to her.
I gave it to her? She seemed to have it from the moment I saw her.
Yessiree, he said, they gots the power. They sitting on it.
Sitting on it?
He looked at me and looked away. She's stronger than you, he let me know.
Hey, I know that, I said, the weaker sex.
Weaker my ass. Why, one pussy hair's strong enough to jerk the Titanic off the bottom of the ocean and sling it all the way to Mars.
What? I said, sticking with it. Is that what it's all about?
He looked at me and looked away. You are a Romeo aren't you?
I didn't say anything. I could hear his bones creak when he got up to walk.

II

I asked him his name once, having stopped a minute where he sat at the corner of Laurel and 12th. As though I might have forgotten or had never been properly introduced, which of course, we hadn't. But it was too soon. He only looked off at the traffic. After a moment, he bummed a cigarette, as if that would be the price for such information.
Lighting it he said, whatever happened to ole Yahwee?
He spoke as if this was some acquaintance neither of us had seen for years.
Yawee? Who I was fairly sure was this other character I used to see him hanging around with walking the streets, but hadn't seen for a while. I said, I don't know, which of course, I didn't.
For a time he wore an old cotton work shirt with *Zeke* etched above the pocket. Odds are it came from the mission or a Good Will bin, but I called him that at another time and he didn't react adversely or surprised, or really react at all. Sometimes I refer to him as *Zeke* when I speak to other people about him, but I've never called him that again to his face.

III

He was sitting under a little tree in back of the alley that runs behind Cumberland Avenue. I was cutting through after eating lunch nearby, making my way back up the hill.
I saw him ahead.
Hey.
He acknowledged me with his eyes and a slight nod but said nothing.
Hot, ain't it? I allowed, sweat pouring off me. He almost nodded again and seemed to hum for a moment.

Guess you're just taking it easy under this tree? I squatted and didn't expect an answer.
Why don't you sit down, take a load off, he offered. That was easily the most inviting he had ever been to me.
Sure, I got a minute. This is a good spot. I noticed he had sort of positioned himself there in the shade. He had an old grocery bag rolled up close beside his crossed legs.
You hungry, I asked. I got part of a sandwich here left over from lunch if you want it. The slightest evidence of a smile seem to affirm and I set it beside his other leg. So, yeah, this is a good place. I guess you come here some? He didn't say anything. I mean, I guess you've come here before.
Before what?
He always surprised me when he'd finally say something and I was never quite sure how to take him. I sensed he didn't mind being difficult, but I wasn't sure that was it.
I guess you were here before?
I guess we all were, he allowed.
Yeah, I reckon. I can roll with that. Good enough, I thought, forget the small talk.
This is before, he said.
Before what? He was starting to lose me, talking and not talking, looking ahead like I wasn't there, humming that little tune I couldn't make out.
Before the tree.

go buy a cantaloupe
sit on the sidewalk
and eat it

jesus is jogging is junk
I'm strung out I can't quit
running praise the lord

Bird Paths

A contrast of bright sun and rich shade
Splayed across an outside staircase
Forgotten rock garden with barren crepe myrtle
Grown together like twisted sculpture where
Mockingbird first appears

No one comes near
But he knows they hear
What will we do, he sings them saying
What can we do, he's heard them before
        Sing! Says Mockingbird holding forth

Even as Crow arrives slinking within earshot
Bivouacked on a chimney stack
Black in the shifting air and changing light
Creaking out his cons and curses
Accepting alms of any pigeons
He purses his beak as if to speak

Sing! Says Mockingbird fluttering up
                to a cluttered gutter
Snatching a moth in mid air
How many starlings must die this day
To mollify screaming Crow? he says
What bough must break so nature's voice is borne?

How many eyes can you pull
    from the city that taught you sight
        and wrought you blind?

Have you given up on Time?
Move the cloud, Monsieur

So the blackbirds with Chinese eyes
Can return to sidewalks and purify the cracks
       that break their mother's backs

Sing! Says Mockingbird to all of these
Lost now in trunks on trains through the redbird Orient
       where coats are torn in doorways
         and children coax their mothers onto window cliffs
              onto floors of foam
       that you must turn to another window
     not to see
      not to learn
       not to fall
Go write your name on the cloud above the wall
Says Mockingbird
On the wall above the cloud

Girls play endless varieties of hopscotch
Between the anarchy of clouds and sidewalks

Who is the man at the window?
No shop owner street vendor
       bike rider rodeo yodeler?
Bid him come and show his ass
That we might pray rain and pass

Who can see the submarine in the tree?
Who can drive such a car with no beak?

Sing! Says Mockingbird
       quoting himself backwards
Sing! he says to the grumbling Cumulous

When will the pool sharks rise up

                    from their envious corners
            and exclaim the wrack of Time?
And claim a keyhole for their wand
Cracking up the new array!
Did you think a white Crow would appear
And steal the wand from your Knoxville Bear?
Make sense man! The bridge trembles
                    with a fish in its belly!

Can the ancient phonograph be recalled?
Have the blackbirds picked your ears clean?

What dove will you uphold?
Under what wing will you bring
Your secret song and sacred word
Your eye of scorn and tattooed lips
To signal the forgotten dance?

Try singing! Says Mockingbird
As the first drops echo down
     and the maestro does a fan dance
          and the crepe myrtle runs screaming
               from the dragon in the sky
Sing! he says 'til the rainbow begins
                    in a stone's eye!

I must die! I must die!
But now I must do

            We don't understand,
say the starlings in unison
He sings in circles, say the sparrows
He's a creep, chime in the chimney sweeps

Listen close, say the jays
                picking pockets with their beaks
We've heard it before, squeak the wrens
                            flitting back in
Ruffling feathers at the weather
Why's there to try?
Who's there to do?
How's there to know?
There's nowhere to go

Watch this! Says Mockingbird
And flies after Crow

How the Daylight fades on the poteau des
refusés, a long shadow climbing walls. The dark shaft
littered with proclamations now a luminescent penumbra
in the dying sun. The rush hour is over. The swishing
traffic subsides. The warm summer shower has ceased
and evaporates in the grace and light of the orange orb
re-emerged in time to disappear beyond the edge of the world.

What could all this mean, besides nothing?

A wooden pole that was once a tree, cut down and drowned
in chemicals, planted in concrete, strung with wires. One
tiny fragment of a vast apparatus that is ultimately a global
system of communication. Its trunk now covered in other
forms of communiqué, visible and penetrated, often legible,
illegal. Their declarations dimmed in the fading light are
suddenly illuminated as a whole and glow in the slanted
rays of sunset.

The scientific mind would render this in ways, the poetic
mind others, the religious mind more again. But what is it,
this *cruel radiance of what is*? How do you answer? What
is the language of perception? Are there symbols and heroes,
is there a method? How does it shape for *you*, old friend?
That is what it is. That and what we don't see and don't
know. Which, I must say, appears to be the most of it.

*The shadows of the pelicans passing over the sand
as I stand looking out to sea stunned by sunlight and
the waves sparkling in one after another as forever
that sound looping back lapping over drifting away
on shimmering memories seemingly buried just there
beneath the swells rising and falling within me on
roads calling me down from hills to coast and back
beating a path midst a wayward map of meanderings
one must only speculate and yet have arrived again
like clockwork like tides to stand and recall beneath
a white sun and shifting sands what has long since
washed away all the old world the old sayings for
the living and there is heartbreak in not knowing not
being able to hold more clearly as though the heat
itself has somehow caught and obscured what was
sought and suspended like a spot on the eye that eludes
focus like a dream that loses shape in broad daylight
and dissipates from the dunes passing into shadows
after you have forgotten what it was that first broke
the light that light that lingers still somewhere bright
in the mind but too far for crossing too far for fear of
drowning as though the night had come with its rumor
of a moon and you must wait for a new sun to wash up
and fresh sands to say what they will and the sea to
sing its song of longing and the dream alive and shining
with its riddle adrift like a faith somehow birthed
and bathed by the sea*

*—Charleston travel journal
Summer of '85*

Lost Pavilion

How Do You Fare old pilgrim of the hills, prodigal child of the wilds? What can you share of your destinies and desires? One cares to know. What 2nd attention, what 4th dimension is among your stray acquisitions? Trailing in from lost horizons beyond the grandfather mountains, arriving through crosswinds and deserts and blinding sea light echoed down this last hallway home. What is it you possess carried over like some pearl in your wandering eye, in your shadow at dusk now…

> *I have returned from the coasts*
> *From the roads and people*
> *I have had my hejira and I dreamed*
> *Of being here of coming back…*
>
> *…I am empty and contented*
> *and I have wandered home*

Coming Upon the old battlefield and taking refuge in a burned out garret of the near abandoned fort, he watched unknown from turrets, spying the ancient magnolias like gravestones…

> *From my window up above*
> *I see the heaps of Babylon*
> *and hear their radio stations*
> *I watch Helen and Alexandria burn*
> *hear the faraway clash of shields*
> *like the clinking of cocktails*
> *toasting the debris of broken seesaws*
> *and Phoenician sails blowing by*
> *half burned upon the breeze…*

He Observed the arrival of foreign merchants who made camp in the valley west of the river. A vast procession of humanity following behind for months to come. Forced to leave the upper rooms he went underground with his illegal lodgings. In a cave below an old stone house he locked himself in beyond the reach of the barbaric throngs and the city rising quickly around him. Maintaining a vigil he worked nightly, pacing the time, seeing the hordes upon themselves...

*what I must do
is to align my actions
with my convictions
lest I bog this swamp
of scams and superstitions
with guilt...*

*...I must go down
go under*

And Then it came, the crashing, the fall, the fast collapse of it all, much as it began. And it was gone. The clearing smoke saw many who were strong were dead. The rest fled, each taking a part of that empire until there was no soul of it left save the ruins running north and south. Random monoliths remained in the withered grasses, deserted stages, shells of dwellings in haste not taken but left to fall, to hold the wind awhile. What God is it shapes this world, he prayed, this Tower of Babel, just to topple every stone? How long do these circles turn? The eye cannot see beyond, he answered, only the river will know the distance. And there in the ruins he made his residence...

The lines are drawn
They are fine with me

The day the night
The long mystery

Is it I who decides
Which way these waterfalls rise

I climb the halls
Only to pass the time

Only to rest on the other side

IN THE FIRST SEASON there came a traveling troupe making their way across the land to a city by the sea. And as they had stopped along the road, he went down to watch them play and hear their stories. An odd and happy assortment they were of men and women and dogs and children. Beneath a mulberry and hackberry whose trunks had grown together into one tree they made their show and drank merrily with those who gathered. Then one among them, the poet called Peter, stood forth at the edge of the street and all of them heard...

A JOURNEY at last unending! A past proceeding.
An avalanche of Time, the eternal moment. Temples
crashing at our heels. Eyes revealing epicanthic folds
where sapota wood breathes and serpent gods guard
doorways to hieroglyphic stairways. Whether great plaza
that long nose rain gods adorn or desert with vision of
rose and oasis, we trace this Road.

O RHAPSODY *of archetypal empathy! Rhythms of the blood. Eruptions through bioregions of time shaking the ladder to its genes. An Americas who rolls down scrolls of parchment, who strolls through parks where ginseng once held court. Clouds blow pyramids by in a tangle of snowy vines. The jungle reclaims what once aimed at the heavens.*

LEAPING NOW *from Doric-like pillars a jaguar with jade spots! Alive on center, entering the modern landscapes, crossing over. A glyph on a monolith on a ley line running twixt seas and polar climes to oracular summits. All creation will follow, as the world on the back of a turtle. All races run for it, not just the leaves rising to the will of the wind. Who will taste the mountain lip untold, who will witness the Delphic centerfold?*

ALLEY DES REFUSÉS. Refuge to expression. Keyhole to a city soul. Assault on protocol, salons of the decadent, academies of the economy. A restructuring of the landscape. Signpost to subtleties overflowed in affirmation of the act. A guerrilla art abruptly exhibiting the world. A lost pavilion where enthusiasts forego the pretense of galleries, publishing companies, reward and compensation, and laws prohibiting and cut through to the original thrust of expression.

What city?
Keyhole city?
T-pole city?
Poet's hole city?
No holds city?
Untold city?

Tic toc town for the taker
        chumped and childless
     chumped and childless

Skyline stuck on a cavesville
        hallowed and honked
              hooped on a hill

Tin town, tit town, town of tunes
Billsville and bildungs too

Park it town. Sunday shut down
Landlord, banker, fireman, mayor
      weathervane flagpole courthouse stairs

Rivertown spilled on a brickville
Walked on glassed out old battlefield

Tarzantown! Tzaraville!
Tarzantown! Tzaraville!

Hush town on hold in a fire drill
Rolled down gay street on square wheels
Throwback, hunchback, halfback (snap)

Teahead town from a sticksville
Ragtime talking up a jazz hound
        barking up the wrong town
Somehow now zip city!

man wants to walk
he ain't got a leash
monkey learns to talk
he got freedom of speech

My Vowels Are Other Colors Than Arthur Rimbaud's

A is red, not black not death
But Alarm
And apple is red
E is green
I is white, wants to be black
But O is snow turning blue
And U, what are you?
U is what comes turning the page

A is Volcano! Fire belching from the belly spewing forth
the flowing lava laying down the garden the bright new
morning fresh from a wrathful god awaking on the wrong
side of bed and life begins.

E the great green growing thing turned on its back and
poking its three legs up through the good crust of earth.
Lights shining through all surfaces and the seeds of poets
to come planted now in the sheen of germs and birds and
fishes glued to future seasons by the yellow sun and
emerald sea.

I speaks in a blizzard! and is a body is somebody else
singing and shining out white as stars and black as
night and all the rainbow prism'd through its gleaming
glowing white eye its godhead of snow!

O the whole world says O I am blue! The sea holding
us in its astral hue swimming through constellations
dipping and rising on mountains and waves and
skyscrapers and careless roads curling through space
a mighty blue O we are.

And U beckons us on to evolve to turn as we must to survive to become God! The one instruction tiny whisper around the corner of unknowing the only secret in the end how we must bend ourselves unto him. U has no color has no meaning maybe doesn't exist.

KNOXVILLE the gray lost in the middle of the alphabet K town somewhere south of the river Ohio and east of the mighty Mississipp lost like the Bermuda Triangle of the Appalachians that gray area of the map that gray matter as yet unused that gray K of Kansas where Dorothy had to come from to go over the rainbow and no place like home and All The Way Home filmed in black and white in Knoxville at the height of the age of technicolor to capture that early century silent movie smoky small town factory feel of Knoxville that still is waking from a two century doze with a bitten lip and bloody nose wearing a cheap B-movie grin and the borrowed clothes of the little tramp's landlord stumbling after some joneses who came through town one time on their way to nowhere and named for the first secretary of war who never set foot here and choked on a chicken bone on a paradox of Knox County who couldn't make up its mind but sided with the Union while its Northern namesake in Maine had Southern sympathies building ships for the slave trade and looking the other way like Rimbaud might of done in some desperation to make money and justify his disproportionate soul looming over the next century where souls still survive and good joes still reside like antique weathervanes waiting for the new world to blow a brave breeze out our way while we while away the glory days on hold for some corporate godot to blow into the territory some Don Quixote on a donkey enterprise come to save us to the greater ranks of modernity and mediocrity which is all the city fathers ever pray for anyway in that occasional sigh set aside for something other than their own good favor and please let us appear as others would have us wherever they may prosperously be hopefully accepting us as themselves in full mutual exclusivity from all those lesser villes until that glorious day we supersede even these and smite them righteously with indignation and appropriation we pray o pray we the gray here that we might be there

Fog Lifted Off the river by mid morning exposing a cityscape like some game board a child forgot to put away. Traffic lurched about in mock seriousness where people paced sidewalks with an employed imperative. At the hour a recorded clock donged the corresponding beats and occasionally issued snatches of music so innocuous as to stalk the zombies plowing their grid. Truly a child at play.

The lunch hour produced a host of flowing bodies from every glass door and store front making their way to lunch counters and tables, a great number of them sitting outside along the concourse and in the sun and shade of the Market Square. Conversation was mannered out to a pitch as construction continued around the side streets. A solitary preacher harangued from a far corner filling in the gaps. In all a great cacophonous air of distraction in face of a perfectly clear blue day.

For no apparent reason rain began to fall from the cloudless sky, the sun boldly shining out. People looked up and then to each other. Their business clothes starting to show the splatter of the shower, which quickly increased in its absurdity bringing steam off the sidewalk and plaza. How in the world could this be, they asked in every way they might as some began to scurry for cover and the rain fell harder from the bright air. The dozer and crane cut off and the dump truck brought to a halt. With that the rain could be heard much greater splashing and soaking everything, plopping food from deserted plates splotching over tables and pavement while the glare of the sun only magnified more surreal.

The street preacher who held steady and oblivious in his public query was now himself drawn to pause watching the herd darting and rushing about with newspapers and pocketbooks above their heads, toppling chairs and bumping into one another. A few poor rain dogs befuddled seeing the masters bolting about them. Now the psalmist too, whose voice every patron had passed by that hour and shunned as it were his weary message, caught up his breath and beheld the unraveling of the mighty scene before him.

He lifted his eyes to that unlikely sky, the wondrous rapture of natural forces, this miracle of sun and rain, and looked upon it.

Then, in a voice that was a stranger even unto himself, he was crying out, *The Devil is beating his wife! The Devil is beating his wife! The Devil is beating his wife!*

And, amazingly, for once, some did believe.

L&N Hotel

We left a few *Hard Knoxville Reviews* scattered in the L&N Hotel, something of a time capsule we imagined at the time of its closing. As usual, we had no idea what time had in mind, not to mention the wayward progressions of art and literature. Unfortunately, I had missed the last night the L&N was open. The woman with the multi-colored eyes who I was so fascinated with at the time later told me she stayed until the end of the evening waiting for me to arrive. Sadly, I was somehow otherwise engaged and didn't make it.

    The L&N Hotel was closed the weekend before the 1982 World's Fair opened, that unprecedented spectacle in the villa of Knox sprawling some 70 acres through the middle of town. The L&N Hotel sat above it all on the north side of the bridge across from the station looking out over the length of the fair grounds down the 2nd Creek valley. For years the L&N Hotel had only been a bar and restaurant, the upstairs with its own back entrance a favorite gathering place for the late-night crowd. Our sincere wish being that it would reopen after the fair had come and gone. However, some time after the fair closed, on a freezing December night between Christmas and New Year's, the old vacant L&N Hotel was burned to the ground. They said it was the bums who started the fire to stay warm. I would at least suspect a few other better-heeled citizens in this crime. I witnessed the violent tragedy from a barely safe distance of six blocks away. Burning boards wafting in an icy night sky drifting over the ruins of the fair site as far as the Sublett Gallery where I stood on the porch. A wall of dense black smoke roiling its way toward me, eventually enveloping all of 11th street to Cumberland Avenue and on to the river to begin the long dissipating trek to the sea. All those nights of a fine piano bar gone up in smoke. All evidence of Thomas Wolfe's letters regarding the exceptional slatterns of a railway boarding house lost for future research. All those kisses in the dark hallway upstairs near the bathrooms, the walks out to the parking lot near the old magnolia tree and the bridge that connected us to our beloved neighborhood. Gone. Now we're left with nothing. Nothing but this, you bums.

Bridge Avenue

There's no bridge on Bridge Avenue

My older brother first pointed this out to me
in an otherwise matter-of-fact conversation
with a slight air of the inexplicable when he
noted this fact

At that time, Bridge Avenue was
seven blocks of a little lane sloping up
from 10th Street
The last three blocks were actually
an alley dead ending into 17th
That longest of the numbered streets, 17th
ascending and descending over the ridge
where General James Longstreet made his
unsuccessful assault on Fort Sanders in 1863
I still contend that 17th should be called
Longstreet

But, there's no bridge on Bridge Avenue
It is a name that projects itself beyond
What the naked eye perceives
Like God or heaven
It suggests a reality that the speculative
Mind must only imagine

This seemed easy enough at the time
And was more or less forgotten

Many years later the city
of Knoxville hosted a world's fair

exhibition which spread itself
over the L&N rail yards
and 2nd Creek valley
that separated downtown
from the hill
where Bridge Avenue began
All the houses on 10th Street
were torn down
It still turned off of Clinch Avenue
by the Candy Factory but then
vanished into a field of temporarily
erected pavilions
When the fair left at the end of summer
10th Street went with it
Officially, it lost its name
And ceased to exist

A few years after this
the Knoxville Museum of Art
manifest itself on the ruins
of the world's fair site
next to the oldest elm tree in the city
which still stood proudly
above the grassy field
When the museum opened
the elm tree died
The street that lost its name
returned extending past
the museum before curving
back into 11th enfolding
a new parking lot
It was named World's Fair Park Drive
Now Bridge Avenue stopped at 11th Street

looking out over the parking lot and the valley
beyond at the foot of downtown Knoxville

Years before this, a rundown apartment
building sat at the corner of 10th
and Clinch across from the Candy Factory
My older brother lived there for awhile
when he was resisting the draft
I used to visit him
We sat on dilapidated old couches
and talked like two old men of the turns
of fate and destiny and lost time
Like 10th Street and the Vietnam War
that apartment building is long gone
and fades from memory

Years later, on a lovely summer evening
I walked up Bridge Avenue with my guitar
and serenaded a girl who lived upstairs
in the house at Bridge and 15th Street
I stood beneath her window and sang
One More Cup of Coffee until she
invited me in

Some years after that, 15th Street
was renamed James Agee Street after
the man who wrote a book about
growing up on Highland Avenue
a half block away from Bridge and
walking with his father downtown
to see Charlie Chaplin movies and
on the way home stopping on the
Asylum Avenue Viaduct to look out

over the rail yards as his father held him
above the trains that rumbled below

When I was a young boy
I sometimes visited my dad's office
at the old L&N Station that sat
like a castle at the end of the viaduct
It was there I first saw a picture
of a naked woman
on a calendar that hung at one
of the many desks spaced beneath
the overhead fans
From the big windows
of that upper floor
You could see all the way down
the rail yard and valley to the Clinch
Avenue Viaduct as well as up the side
slope to the houses and trees
of 10th and 11th Street

One spring day so many years later
I sat in that office filling out employment
forms to work track maintenance on
a section gang for the L&N Railroad
Looking out those same windows
to the houses and streets I had been
wandering around all winter
I felt as though I was crossing over
from one world into another

My father worked 36 years
for the L&N Railroad
and remembers when Hollywood
came to town and made a movie

of James Agee's book
He watched take after take
of Jean Simmons running down
the hill from 10th Street
chasing the little boy who
played little Agee

At about this same time, a few
blocks away on Highland Avenue
James Agee's real boyhood home
was bulldozed to make room for
a small apartment building

It was just a few years ago
I walked into the Graduate Library
on White Avenue a couple of blocks
down from Bridge between 13th
and 15th streets and came upon
an old hand drawn map of
Knoxville circa 1880's
The ramparts of the Civil War fort
still dominated the top of the hill
to the west of town but a quilt
of roads and trees and houses had
begun to spread up to it
White, Clinch, Laurel, Bridge and
Highland Avenues were all there
only Laurel was called Grove
and Highland was called Cedar
The cross roads weren't numbered
but had names: Morrow, Scott, Blount
John, Ann, Dickinson, and Temple
Where 17th would one day rise
over the ridge it now only began

at Old Kingston Pike and pushed
a little ways up the hill toward
the fort as Fort Sanders Avenue
On the north side the L&N
Station was yet to be built
but south down the valley
Clinch Avenue was already the main
connector crossing over with its
long straight bridge into town

Here were the very beginnings
of the Fort Sanders neighborhood
With close inspection you could
trace the old roads and see how the
modern grids were founded
Crossing the 2nd creek valley and
moving west of town each of the new
roads trailed to an end as they
approached the fort at the crest of the west ridge
Beyond that was only a sweep of
fields and countryside waiting
for future developers
Moving back along those short new roads
each came to a halt at Morrow
which would later be 10th
the edge of the high ground
before it dropped off into the valley
where there was a single railroad
track and a creek with no given name
Bridge was only five blocks then
From Morrow to Dickinson
which would later become 15th
and even later be James Agee Street
But then I noticed that Bridge

only appeared to stop at Morrow on
the high edge of the valley with the other roads
and that the cut away of land
in the drawing obscured the detail
of how it picked back up as it
made its way past where the old elm
tree would have been standing
and on down into the valley crossing
the solitary track and then
the creek by way of a very small
bridge

A few years from now
at the corner of James Agee Street
and Laurel Avenue where
a house burned down long ago
an asphalt parking lot will be reclaimed
and turned into a small memorial park
dedicated to James Agee
The park will back up to Bridge Avenue
just a half block from where
Agee's boyhood home stood
And there in the park
magnificent old magnolia trees
will stand guard like gallant sentries
over the grassy essence of those slopes
rooted like ancient gravestones in the hill
helping to hold the memories of
lost souls and lost houses
lost streets and lost wars
and lost bridges

When My Brother Comes Stumbling

When my brother comes stumbling
                            drunk on proclamation
Happy to pronunciate, elucidate this
                        fine day's good fate
Elated saint taking liberty
Spectacled fellow who looks like yeats
                                drinking li po

THIS HOUSE IS MADE OF STONE
WALK AN ANGEL ROUND THE BLOCK
CALL THE GOV'NOR ON THE PHONE

Dancing with the cactus
                out of practice
Hillbilly haiku preacher poesy
O Southern progeny
O happy mistake
        how made me

PRAISE BE TO DIONYSUS
AND HIS BROTHER BACCHUS
FROM WHOM ALL NECTAR FLOWS

Remember what you say today
                        good brother
        O Bamboo Valley Idler
It's a new year
The early version for the early bird

I'M THE EARLY WORM HERE
CONSIDER IT
CONSIDER ALL THE WARM SOUNDING

SOUTHERN CITIES

Beautiful Beaufort by the sea
Twenty-six miles from Yemasee

FIGHT FOR A WARMER WORLD

Suburban Bourbon
South Savannah

SEWANEE RIVER ROLLING DOWN THE PIANO

To be sure big brother
Now slide me down that big glass bar
I'm twelve today all mellowed up
No dull elixir here great man

WE'LL SIT HERE 'TIL THE ROBINS GO CORRUPT
'TIL THE SPARROWS ROLL UP THE BEER
      BARRELS AND THE COWS COME
            TRICKLING IN

The Doc may be here soon

TELL THE DOC TO SHOOT THE MOON
NO TELL THE DOC YES
TELL THE NURSE SHE'LL HAVE TO GUESS

Here drink this
Straight off the lizard's tail

STRAIGHT UP A DUCK'S PAW
O IDLEWILD SOUTH
O HORSES MOUTH

THERE'S EARS ON THAT BIRD

So I've heard

SO I HAIL

Now pass that word along
           and sing that song to me

AND SEND THAT CROW MY WAY

And if I sing a loony tune
I only mock the autochthonous squawk
                      of yonder hills

JUST GETTING MY FILL

Comfort in the River, good brother

EZRA BROOKS AND TW SAMUELS
WERE FIGHTING IN THE CAPTAIN'S TOWER

Were FLOWING in the captain's tower

ONE SAID TO THE OTHER
I'M DRUNK AT THIS HOUR

Father Fisheye

The great crowd was leaving le Grande Dérangement
emptying out into the streets of old Quebec. But you
turned and walked back, making your way through a
sea of chairs in the semi-dark. Your shoulder bag and
cane in hand. I thought at first you were maybe drunk,
but saw you were only limping as you came over to
our table and sat down and started talking. Your face
in the candlelight.

Father Fisheye
All of my life
Is just the blink of an eye
Is that your hand on my thigh?

Later, after the film of you and Peter and Lafcadio,
you came running down the hall saying, tell me what
did you think, what did you think of it? I said I found it
a little frightening although I was amazed at all you did,
all the places, the cities, the scenes. You said, yes,
sometimes it's hard for me to believe everything I've
been through, and all that we become. Then a young
girl held up a portrait she'd just drawn of you.

Father Fisheye
Who are the best minds?
And then the people were there
You turned to preach to the choir:
Everything's holy, everything's blessed
Here in this moment where it manifests
Yes, here on the Plains of Abraham
On the Plains of Abraham
On the Plains of Abraham

Well, the whole affair was a feast of passion, and a
minor victory for the Québécois. The Latin Quarter
was electric and overflowing with the many tribes.
The St. Lawrence would forever be the River Muse.
Le Conférence de Kerouac, another international coup.
But it was late, late in the game. October for the King
of May, as you prepared to fly back to Boulder and
Buddha and the rest of the century.

And routines up in a room
All your friends will be here soon

Father Fisheye
I am I
I am the worm at your ear
I crossed the seas just to be here:

There is no future, there is no past
It's always now, but it never lasts, it never lasts
No, but it's good to eat for a thousand years
Good to eat for a thousand years
Good to eat for a thousand years

Reverie Written on my Back While Lying in the Grass at the Jack Kerouac Memorial in Lowell, Mass

    Are these yellow gladiolas?
    Are they glad for the bees to ogle them?
    Are those seagulls flying over Lowell?
    On my back in the shade of a little oak
    Letting the word sift through to me
    From migrating clouds headed south
    Whose path I cross
    Whose boss is my boss in this world
    This spherical curl of existence
    This persistent heart of life
    The rata tat tum twinkle of the cups
    Held up to catch the sun
    They play to the passing clouds who
    Peek at me too
    All present and accounted for
    All gone daddies
    O Gladiola Day

    Just cloud gazing
    This in front of that in front of that
                           in front of what?
    Will the clouds clear?
    Who are they?
    A centipede, a scorpion, a president falling apart
    A wisp of a wafting word stretching
    Into other words
    A drifting thought over that willow
    Who's so weary of reaching out
    But now, just now, just the blue
    The blue and you

And if a cupped leaf at the top of a tree
Catches the sun and holds it
Who's holding who?
The blue observes
My back to the good earth
Old dead Jack's turf
That Indian thing
And only the birds know the words
Little sparrows of Lowell
Serenading a migrating crow

And when I looked again, Mr. Cumulous
Was introducing us to Time, sir
And there's a little water in the parlor of Time
A little contemplation of precipitation
Held up for examination
Out of focus fuzzy edge of dissipation
And the wind comes in singing
Saying, nothing ever changes

And this is where we started
With a mere wisp appearing
Fluffing fulfilling stringing out
A small white dragon gone into the leaves
The past, you might say, the thin air
Just a few words written there
Who no one can read
What kind of mind would it take to read that?

The birds start to talk again, feeling assured
A worm in the beak is no time to speak
But a worm in the belly is a whole new story

Is there no end to the parade of puffs?
How long have we been coming?

White faces pressed against the blue
Where rain once pressed a date
Wind strewn eyes from sockets rise
To find another face
And cotton weeps above the streets
Of wine and time-worn shoes
Don't stop me wondering skyward
To shape these whites and blues

Have I scared away the people
Who would read the monuments?
The birds have lost their fear of me
And light on low branches above
I hear the horns of the city
The long reach of the sun is splintering
The leaves and my lashes
Gradually arcing down the tree and
Finding my shade and me
I had fallen asleep

My most lost moment
Found out by the sun
Who can you trust?
Trust Jack, dead but true
In his word
I rise up and an old black lady
Is walking across the grass
My old Indian hair hangs across my face
Filled with dirt and woodchips and grass
No way to say what fills my eyes

What fills my soul?
I guess old Indian hair
Dirt and wood and grass
Clouds and blue sky

The University of Tennessee Revisited

How weird to walk the halls of a university again
A stranger, a spy I am
Not only the dropout, the outsider
But also from another time
A different day of learning
My one poor year spent burning
                      the candle for peace
Staging a strike, studying the people,
                          dodging police
William Knustler, Phil Ochs, Circle Park
Billy Graham, Dick Nixon, Neyland Stadium
No nostalgia for me
I learned a few things

It was all in passing
And still passing it seems

But don't I carry with me some of those days
And some from long before?
I learned something early on
I found it in daydreams and broken crayons
The melody of sky and earth
A hidden voice
The hot breath of running free
And what good has it done me?
And what of all those pages turned
                          and paths gone down?

I became a cloud dreamer, book reader,
soul singer
A sun chaser and great loafer
Like Adam in the garden

Like Whitman in America
A student of the stone
I called myself those many moons ago
Upon the eve of leaving formal schooling
Nearly 30 years now rolling that stone
And what can be said of all that AWOL?
Well, no regrets
None that I would mention
I've learned a few things
              a few things in passing
But one walk down that long echoed corridor
The painted block walls, the lockers
And all is recalled from before and after
The stone, the wall, the endless hallway out

I'm Supposed to say
It's May and mild
And I'm sitting outside
At the Café k'Ville
With no one beside me
In this black shirt I still
Haven't washed

I'm supposed to point out
That the night is young
Or the season is changing
Or the war is on
Or maybe just go into some
Political comedy

I'm supposed to be here now
And establish the possibility
Of you joining me

After which, we can have a drink
And await the slanderous air
Of those less bored
and less committed
Which will only sooth the sow's ear

We may even be encouraged
They may even buy the next round
They may say please!

We just want you to relax and think
Which we can easily fake

underman

what i must do
is to align my actions
with my convictions
lest i bog this swamp
of scams and superstitions
with guilt

and for what is poetry
what occurs in words
attempt an honesty
that is built
both of will and chance
of suspended memory
and happy accident

like one who dons
deep sea diving gear
or the headdress of an astronaut
the village boy who
climbs the highest tree
on the highest hill
and comes back to tell
of the witness beyond

i must go down
go under
swing so low
my vehicle will vanish

into a point will explode
into a keyhole of
the soul

i must do
what i didn't do
before i fled
i must shed
this skin
and begin

CITY OF BRUSH FIRES, burning houses, lost rivers. A pot stirring in the backwash of drowned souls. Origin of some, last outpost of others. Bermuda Triangle of the Appalachians. Caves beneath the river. Pagan art hanging off buildings. Abstract dispatches jamming up telephone poles. Dreams, like paintings on alley walls. Zurich 1916. The wailing of the primordial intellio modern. History may visit, but you can't go home again. There are no Meccas, only waiting lines. This is naked city.

AND THE SUN comes up, and the Specter reappears, like a barnacle on the hull of the thing. Some of the fires keep burning. I imagine writing a letter.

GLIMPSE OF A MANIFESTO. Notion of affirmation. Declaration of undoing. Idea of form. Nameless, but names appear. Like a glass bead game, ultimatum infinitum. Wisdom of chance. Negative space focus. X factor deviled up through Finnegan. History being lover and mother to the artist. Both having moved away. Ob-la-di Ob-la-dada. A new game of go with silly no rules.

A BASEMENT STUDIO in an alley off 8th Street, bunkered in the tomb of the Ottoman Empire, with all the godhead gear. No clock present, just the cooings of Salome louder than Stalin, and an invisible wheel. The rusty metal door between this and the outside world opens from within and the Field Master stands at the threshold with a freshly struck cigarillo, the lit tip pointing upwards to a blazing sky. He is way up in music.

"We have some intellectual property we wish to rezone commercial," he proposes as though someone was out there listening. The deceptive February sun streams in with the lovely noise of the world and occasional wafts of Lee's Chicken. Rising from the shadows behind him a concrete floor splattered with paint, a few odd rugs, a couple of couches, black curtains covering the walls. A closet booth for vocals. The drums and bass and electric guitars all stationed out in the open. Off to one side the soundboard and accompanying machines with a jungle of wires growing out of them. Flickering there on a spliced piece of film is the engineer, a scientist on a chain with wise hands and blinking lights in his eyes. He works the wrenches on the tanks, tightening the tracks, greasing the triggers. His assistant, a young monk from Texas, shuffles between microphones and amplifiers adjusting all things inward and upward.

"Where are the teen witches?" the Field Master inquires, secretly pleased that all the montys and haints and tree surgeons are absent from the killing fields. Dug in for two days, personnel have been deployed and artillery brought forward. Strewn among the snakes of cables, open guitar cases full of nuclear waste, makeshift drum cymbal lampshades, and Christmas lights leftover from Fab Four displays, the troops are stirring. An odd cast of irregulars, part of a lost guard, a little scarred for the revolving. Minutemen who were never defeated but never made it home to march the row of a hit parade. Outcast divinity scholars, outsider anthropologists, world-class Okies, Colorado sharpshooters, salvation army transplants made good, New Englanders, Louisiana boys, volunteers from Tennessee. And one remarkable woman who refused to go to safety and stayed on 'til the end to go down with her husband.

It is a war, alright. But like Jerry Lee said, "What did you think a record was anyway, just a little thing that goes round and round?"

The big wheel is turning, like a child playing in the yard, like a soldier walking by the side of the road on the outskirts of some foreign town. The big wheel turns and swallows the world, puking up scenes that have been seen again and again, connected cogs, derivative sounds, passion plays playing out over and over, and wars and rumors of wars warring on unto the stars.

And what? No ground is held for long. It all turns over like wheat, like death and taxes. The brains scatter, the skin bloats. The doves come back when the smoke clears. And what? Another deal is struck. The usual suspects. Some prima donna on the ramparts, her lips slightly parted, launching a thousand ships in the direction of another gift horse. Or some Zeke throwing stones, crying wolf! Some tatterdemalion cloudpisser gone a-hunting for a grace note. Yea and verily. A refugee of some rank, exiled behind enemy lines in a music city where all the maps are on fire.

The Field Master secures the hatch, turns and scopes the vantages, eyes squinted in 5th Century Chinese. A battered flag of some archaic dynasty about his neck, a cravat against the winds of egregious trends and hong kong moments and otherwise artifacts unwanted.

"The siege of Malta was the worst," he confesses, "I don't know how men did that."

He can't dither a wheel, he can't dink a millisecond, he can't read directions. But give him something with knobs and tubes. Give him the jawbone of an ass. Ever since Tommy Clapton told that lie, shades of lycanthrope bristle his judgment. A howling of searchlights unchecked in the wolfer night.

"It's hot in this booth," a singer intones.

"Think of the slaves building the pyramids," the Field Master suggests as he tunes the air a final time.

And then, a signal. A countdown. The bloom swells disembodied, vaporous plumes of sound resounding. A litany of weepings, exclamations, charms and aggressions. The wheel appears, then reappears at a different angle, rolling over the left flank, dredging up old graves and Tommy Lanois sirens in the cemetery air. The bombardment begins. Drums bursting in air! Firing squad confessions, foxhole manifestoes looking for a pulse. The tetanus shot guitar. Salome re-enters with red-winged blackbirds sailing before her. You realize now she's been wailing all along. She falls asleep on the couch and starts to dream aloud. Madmen with money follow. They try to wake her, to buy her, to sell her. There's an explosion in the booth. The roof gives, and the front wall caves in.

"The hellcats are upon us!" the young monk screams.

"Let the hellcats come," says the Field Master, "their wolfman waits."

He stands in the rubble with a Spanish guitar, a scientist in swaddling clothes. One foot upon the rock, the other on the floor. The wheel within a wheel now spinning out like a force field, like a mighty shield.

Silence falls upon the ethers. Take one.

"Where are they?" muffled voices arise.

"They're nowhere," says Salome who wakes up and starts handing out reviews. The troops begin to emerge. The Field Master removes his headgear. The engineer looks to him for instruction. He gives the signal and says, "Let's move forward."

Amazingly, the stars are out. There is a war, but there is no enemy. No enemy to be seen, just the echoes receding and the endless sky revolving like a big broken wheel. You realize now, they can never defeat you, but only knock your walls down.

About the Book

Bembo was modeled on typefaces cut by Francesco Griffo for Aldus Manutius' printing of *De Aetna* in 1495 in Venice, a book by classicist Pietro Bembo about his visit to Mount Etna. Griffo's design is considered one of the first of the old style typefaces, which include Garamond, that were used as staple text types in Europe for 200 years. Stanley Morison supervised the design of Bembo for the Monotype Corporation in 1929. Bembo is a fine text face because of its well-proportioned letterforms, functional serifs, and lack of peculiarities; the italic is modeled on the handwriting of the Renaissance scribe Giovanni Tagliente. Books and other texts set in Bembo can encompass a large variety of subjects and formats because of its quiet classical beauty and its high readability.

COVER PHOTOGRAPH:
Karly Stribling took this photograph
after a fire that destroyed the Pickle Mansion,
an iconic house in the Fort Sanders neighborhood.

Design by Robert B. Cumming, Jr.

—Tinah Utsman

RB MORRIS, poet, singer, songwriter, musician, and playwright, hails from Knoxville, Tennessee. In the 1980's he edited an arts and literary tabloid, *Hard Knoxville Review*, which attracted a cult following in this country and in Europe. He is widely published as a poet. He also wrote a one-man play, *The Man Who Lives Here Is Loony* (1992), taken from the life and work of writer James Agee, and recently played Agee in productions of the play both at the University of Tennessee and at the Cornelia Street Café in NYC. In recent years Morris has been a celebrated recording artist. His CDs include *Local Man, Take That Ride, Knoxville Sessions, Zeke and the Wheel,* and *Empire*. Morris is currently the Writer-in-Residence at the University of Tennessee.

For more information visit:
www.rbmorris.com

www.ingramcontent.com/pod-product-compliance
Lightning Source LLC
Chambersburg PA
CBHW032121090426
42743CB00007B/421